The Passion of the Right-Angled Man

The Passion of the Right-Angled Man

Poems by
T. R. Hummer

University of Illinois Press
Urbana and Chicago

Publication of this work was supported in part by grants from the National Endowment for the Arts and the Illinois Arts Council, a state agency.

Manufactured in the United States of America

This book is printed on acid-free paper.

Some of these poems appeared previously in various magazines and are reprinted by permission:

Ascent: The Passion of the Right-Angled Man
Hudson Review: First Love, When It Falls; Love Song; A Fool Is a Man Who Understands Nothing but Remembers Everything; Drowning, *A Ghost Story*
Memphis State Review: Passion, Circumstance, What I Gave to the Air; Or, If You Were Closer, I Might Touch You; The Lost Woman
New England Review: The Age before Passion, *A Vision;* Love Poem, *The Possessed;* Cruelty
New Jersey Poetry Journal: Genealogy
The New Yorker: Dawn: What I Might Have Dreamed; Love Poem, *The Dispossessed*
Poet and Critic: Because You Will Not Let Me Say I Will Love You Forever
Prairie Schooner: Train Wreck, 1890: My Grandmother Lies Down with the Dead
Quarterly West: The Beating; Correspondence: Faded Love
Texas Review: Any Time, What May Hit You; Sorrow; Going In, *A Prayer for the Others;* A Kindness
Western Humanities Review: Coming Back, False Dawn

Library of Congress Cataloging in Publication Data

Hummer, T. R.
The passion of the right-angled man.

I. Title.
PS3558.U445P3 1984 811′.54 84-8607
ISBN 0-252-01130-9

for Theo,

for my mother and father,

and for Dave Smith and Gordon Weaver,
teachers and friends

CONTENTS

I

Coming Back, False Dawn 3

Circumstance: The Dismantling 4

The Age before Passion, *A Vision* 7

Love Poem, *The Possessed* 10

First Love: When It Falls 12

Any Time, What May Hit You 15

Because You Will Not Let Me Say
I Will Love You Forever 16

Cruelty 17

A Fool Is a Man Who Understands
Nothing but Remembers Everything 19

The Beating 21

Passion, Circumstance, What I Gave to the Air 22

The Passion of the Right-Angled Man 24

Dawn: What I Might Have Dreamed 25

Traps 27

Or, If You Were Closer, I Might Touch You 34

Love Song 35

The Lost Woman 37

II

Love Poem, *The Obsessed* 41

Genealogy 43

Correspondence: Faded Love 44

Train Wreck, 1890: My Grandmother
Lies Down with the Dead 52

The Oracle of the Lonely Man
in Stillwater, Oklahoma 54

Those, Trespassing 55

Drowning, *A Ghost Story* 60

Love's Mercy and the Dark World Dying 64

Circumstance: The Vanishing 68

Flying Away 72

Going In, *A Prayer for the Others* 74

Sorrow 76

A Kindness 78

Love Poem, *The Dispossessed* 79

I did not know what was happening in my heart.
—Robert Penn Warren

I

COMING BACK, FALSE DAWN

So it is morning this time, early, the sun not over
Eastern mountains, light rising in a long false dawn,
Valley deep in shadow, gold just starting to color
Peaks, clouds, air. It is nearly a year since I walked on
This path into foothills, half drunk, stumbling, driven
By a woman's body, by the drift of a life gone wrong,
By love. It was night, and a moonset turned the mountain
White—my skin glowed in that light and I thought I was blessed
Not, God knows, with vision in a high place, but with passion,
And when the moon went under, I touched my own face in darkness,
Thought *Passion is everything*. It might have been
Starlight, it might have been one last glimmer out of the west,
Moonlight thrown off a cloud from behind the horizon—
But I thought I saw, in the air above me, a woman's face
Shine for a moment, then turn away, gone.
Say it was moonlight on stone. Say it was time and place
And a man unhinged by love. Say it was circumstance.
I'll believe anything. That night I believed it was grace,
And a man who'd think that doesn't stand a chance.
It's not here this morning. I've come back alone
With day behind mountains, night in the valley—balanced
Now, I try to see past circumstance, past passion
Whose face I believed I might touch in this gold of false dawn.

CIRCUMSTANCE: THE DISMANTLING

Morning: in the square of the window, light:
A square of sun on the bare
Floor of the room: that,
And a light-colored square in the corner
Where something massive sat years
Holding back the darkening

Of dirt from its span of floor:
Vanity: I see her face
Years younger in the streaked
Silver of the beveled mirror, her hair
Fallen from its height of habitual bun:
She in her squareness of flesh and long nightgown

Brushing: her back to me: the tarnished back
Of the square silver brush the same
Color as the hair it moves through,
And in this room, lit only by the small
Glow of bedside lamp, the live blue
Sparks jump out of her brushing:

I stand in the door, a smaller
Body than she is, watching her face
Watch itself in the mirror, jowled flesh
Loose and quivering at her throat, her stare
Upward and vacant, oblivious
Of me or the years my being there

Define: the strong even strokes
Of old brush counting toward this light
Where I lean again in the squared doorframe
We heft the dark old vanity through,
Uncles and cousins wrestling
Its clumsy corners out into the bed

Of a pickup while the aunts drag
Box after box out of cabinets
To sift through photographs, crumbling
Clippings, diplomas, letters
With squares cut in corners,
Stamps vanished into somebody's closet album:

Funeral announcements still black-edged years
After nobody knows who the dead are:
Aunts and cousins and daughters sorting
And saying, low-voiced, all they can
And cannot remember: and I remember
She looks down at me, says *Son*

Can't you sleep, and I shake
My head, and she says *That's all right,*
Neither can I, you just lie
In my bed yonder and count
While I brush: I lie in that yonder, the hollow
Her body's years of weight

Have pressed in the mattress: her hand
Moves, and I count, and the dark
Comes and goes so many times I do not know
What numbers to call it,
The room emptying itself
Of everything but light:

And it would be easy to stop
Now, easy to end with light
And an empty room, the neat cliché: easy
Not to say I have a daughter
I do not live with, and she sleeps
Or does not sleep in whatever dark

She comes to: easy to forget
I am in this room a man
My grandmother would not know
How to talk to, how to look at square in the old
Mirror of the vanity I come back to
Again and again, wanting someone

To tell me *I love you*
Anyway, no matter what
Has fallen to pieces in any dark,
No matter what you say.

—for my grandmother, 1885–1979

THE AGE BEFORE PASSION

A Vision

In the honey-rich light
Of July Louisiana sun
I see the old
Ford truck bump over the white
Shell road from Hammond

Loaded down
With what sounds like the mutter
Of distant thunderheads,
With a smell dense as ozone
On a night when heat lightning flickers:

A beeyard on wheels,
Stacked high with live
Hives and empties, frames
And foundations, all
The gear you need to give

Bees their care and breeding.
The truck darts in and out
Of shafts of light shot through
Live-oak limbs, light bleeding
Brilliance from the stacked hives, white

And blinding in that air:
Air full of the smell
Of river, the Tangipihoa,
A name obscure
And unpronounceable

To Mississippi boys just over
The line for the first time in their lives,
Two of them, both in khaki,
My uncle and my father.
They are young, their children, their wives

Undreamed of. My father is sixteen.
My uncle, older, drives.
My father's face is grave,
Eyes squinting with wind as he leans
Out the truck window. Behind him, hives

Hum. He hears them,
Turns his head so his ear
Is closer to the slow pulse,
The old dark rhythm
Like heartbeat. The river is near,

And as he turns, a great
White waterbird, egret, rises
From hiding, lifts
Out of oaks. My father's heart
Is quiet. He tries

To follow the egret's flight,
Looks up. I see his head
Tilt against the pure
Glowing white
Of hive behind him, silhouetted,

Eclipsed. If I could see
His face, it would be beautiful
With the peace of his unknowing.
But in the obscurity
Of that brilliance, I only behold

The strong line of jaw, nose,
Hair blown back, blown wild,
Mouth open a little as though
He wants to speak. But no
Words come. I see his dark profile

Light suddenly as the truck
Enters a shadow, shades
Hives from sun. His eyes
Are closed. He looks
Like a man who has just prayed

For something his life is not
Worth a prayer without.
But he has not prayed.
He would not know what
To pray for. He would not

Believe me if I could tell him.
On the road a mile ahead
Is a town. He's going there:
Springfield. It will seem
Like any town he's sweated

To set up a beeyard in.
But that dark-haired fourteen-year-old
Girl across the street
Will watch with strange fascination
As he puts his gloves on, holds

The veil ready. Their eyes will meet.
He will put the beeveil on,
Go to work. The girl is my mother.
She will stand on her side of the street
A long time before she goes home

Wondering why she can hear
Blood beat in her ears so clearly,
What that slow rhythm is,
Why birds cry so loud on the river,
Why the sun is so low so early.

—for my father and mother

LOVE POEM

The Possessed

If I dream of this water again,
This pond, clear
Eye of the earth staring up at me
Green and amazed
With the shape of wind,
I will have to stand here
As I always do, changed
By dreaming into a boy
Who has to lean, look down,
Stare back, no matter what face

Swims up out of bottom-muck.
But it is not a dream, it is
The pond where my father's cattle
Come, go out belly-deep
In August heat, water warm as blood
In the green-stained shade of willows.
I am here. I can touch
This water, see small bass dart
In shallows, hear a kingfisher's whistle
And the low plop

A turtle makes going under.
It is all as I would remember
If I were remembering, if I were
Somewhere else, my body the strange
Changed shape of a man,
If I were a man asleep in some other
Life, dreaming this dream
That sooner or later will be
About the woman. A boy does not
Have that, has only the long

Hot stretch of afternoon,
Does not yet know
The night, the touch of a hand
On his face that will turn
The wind around, make the sun
Slant, darken the pond so
When I finally lean and look down
I cannot see
If her face the water always holds
Looks back at anything, anyone.

FIRST LOVE: WHEN IT FALLS

Red in the east, through the crack
In the curtain—I wake
In the room I have waked in
Every day of my life, now not knowing
Where I am. Sleep has not lost me.
Dreams have not. I look down
At my arms, thin on the sheet,
Wonder at the shape my body

Takes on the bed. I stir, throw
The covers back, open the curtain, stare
At the great dewy web cantilevered
From window screen to eave, the orb-spider,
Size of my hand, hung there, black against red
Phosphorescence of dawn,
That dark eight-pointed star
Not moving, or turning so slow

I cannot see it spin.
I hear my father and mother
Speak softly, not to wake me.
I cannot hear what they say.
It is summer, I am a boy
Thirteen, awake in the strange
Dawn light, awake in the room
The world does not know I have waked in,

The room I do not know is mine.
My mother's voice in the kitchen
Has no more words in it
Than the lowing of cattle coming
From the distant field, from the pond
Where they drink dark water
Before light. I can see, in this red
Sunrise, their black shapes far

Across pasture. I know
What they are. *How do I know?* My hands
Move, touch the screen, not an inch
From the silver of web—
The spider, high on the edge
Near the roof, feels my touch,
Raises one leg, shakes it
Free of a clinging strand,

Poises. I hear
My mother's skillet ring, touched
By a spoon. The sound is like light
Sudden on water. I remember
The rod in my hand, the silver
Arc of the fish, my father
Saying *Slow, don't jerk, give it line:*
The line, colorless, glowing

Out with the dive the fish takes
Before rising, breaking water again.
I see the shape of my hand,
Strange to me, jiggle the screen,
See the spider lift, fall from the web,
Swing out on its line, swing in
To the center, see the center shake
As my hand shakes, see

The spider hang on, black
Silhouette scrambling against
The stillness of dawn—I think
Look, I have touched
The thing! Yes, touched it
With this hand that must be mine
Because it has touched. The web
Still trembles. I touch my own

Face, feel fingers light
Against flesh, the way
My mother's hand feels
When it comes out of darkness,
And I, half sleeping, know
She is there, I am here: but now
It is my own hand, my own face,
And it is not sleep

I am lost in. Alone
In this room that does not belong
To me, room spun around me,
I swing suddenly free
Of the love that has held me
Still in the world, and I fall
Out, dark against dawn's glow,
Holding on to the bright thin thread

Of myself, almost nothing, ready to break.

ANY TIME, WHAT MAY HIT YOU

The foreman whacks him hard
In the back of the head and calls him
Dumbass because he is lost
In the dream of the woman he touched
Last night and lets the milk can slip.
It goes over in a sudden
Explosion of white,
The Holsteins jerk in their stalls,
And the foreman swings
Before the clatter has time to stop.

He lies there a long time after
The foreman stomps out cursing,
Lies flat on his belly
In a puddle of milk, watching one
White rivulet vanish
In the concrete dung-trough.
The cattle stop their bucking
And the barn goes still:
The milk, udder-warm, soaks through
His shirt and he shakes
His head to stop the spinning, feeling
The hand on him sudden
Out of the dark, the wordless
Breath, the lurch
The world took at her touch:
The letting go, the spilling.

BECAUSE YOU WILL NOT LET ME SAY I WILL LOVE YOU FOREVER

I go out into ninety-proof moonlight
Alone, drive home alone, dangerous to the world.
The world recognizes me like this, tight
And comic in my perilousness. At the party, a girl
Half-dressed and -drunk and wondrously endowed
With tit-shaking hiccoughs, begged me for a cure. I told
Her and everybody else around I had it straight from God,
The gift of the laying on of hands. I put my palm
Hard on her forehead, yelled *Spirits, begone!* so loud
She choked on her gin-and-tonic. When she grew calm
From the terror of that exorcism, she proclaimed me
A prophet, a true Son, and asked me to take her home.
Ah, but the way home is not straight, is long and deadly
And she is not with me—I sicced her on a willing friend—
And you are not. You were not even at the party,
Having other fish to fry, your own long darkness to descend.
I concede that. The world and I concede some things
Together: moonlight, starlight, the way the front end
Of the car weaves mystically: the world, in fact, sings
Its compromise in the weird blood that beats in my ears:
Get out and walk. Give it up. But no: there are sufferings
Too precious, confusions too great to surrender
No matter who says to, no matter what prophecy
Comes to me out of the dark: and this is what we are
As long as I won't believe it, as long as I am too far gone to see
What things are possible, what things the world will not let be.

CRUELTY

It was a dare that made us break
Into the locked storeroom where the sweet
Dust we raised coming shone
In the door's shaft of light.
My brother took me deep
In the dark of heaped junk
My grandfather left there knowing
It was good and someone would want it,
Someone would need to touch it,
Find something there he could name:
Gloves. Beeveil. Smoker.

My brother brought them out
Of those shadows, put them on me,
And I stood there strange to myself
Holding the lamp of the smoker
As he filled it with pinestraw, struck it
With fire, fitted the lid.
Then the smell of pinesmoke rose
Out of my hands, and he led me
Into the grove, the ruined
Beeyard. My brother
Held my arm and we heard

The hum in the air, saw the quick
Gold bodies flash
Through swaths of shadow and sun.
You know what you said you'd do,
He told me. *I dare you.*
That morning I was not half
As tall as a man, had never torn
Anything open, never touched
What sweetness a man might find,
But when my brother pushed me
I could only stumble

To the nearest hive, lay my hand
On the lid, feel
Its pure presence, white
As the body of the woman I would not
Come to for years: I stood there afraid
Of what I could not stop
From doing, afraid my heart
Would choke on its own
Thick blood: and I knelt
To touch the slit
Where the bees came, bodies

Dusted with pollen, glowing.
Smoke, my brother yelled, *smoke!*
I raised all the heat I could hold,
All the fire he had given me, knowing
The power of that one
Word, *dare:* not the bitter
Incense of passion, not the gold
Stunned clustering of bodies
In the dark my grandfather put there:
Needing to know, but not knowing
The pain, what flesh would come to

When I ripped off the lid.

A FOOL IS A MAN WHO UNDERSTANDS NOTHING BUT REMEMBERS EVERYTHING

It is a long time now since the blue
Of the arc-light etched
Handprints of maple leaves
Black on the sidewalk.
There was rain.

I was a stupid man.
I did not know what it meant
That we were there together,
Did not know we were held

In the shape light makes
When it touches something.
I thought I was drunk.
It was raining, and it seemed
A drunk thing to do

To stand under trees in the rain.
I don't know what you thought
You were, not even now,
But when you touched my face

There must have been
A shadow under your hand.
There must have been light
Coming down from behind you
Or I would not remember you

Glowing that way,
Something only a fool
Would think could happen.
But I know there was rain

On your hand, I know your hand was light
On my face. I was not
Drunk or stupid then,

But I was still a fool.
I did not reach for you.

I let you stand
Touching me, an arm's length away,
Knowing the shadow we threw
Was a shape I had never seen,

One I could change.

THE BEATING

Everybody knew Clifton Cockerell was not half bright,
But nobody knew his passion
Till we found him on the playground back of the junior high
Carving names on a tree. His poor secret
Stood no more chance of staying one

Once we had it, than Clifton did of knowing
Why we cared—but we couldn't let it rest
Till everybody heard it, especially the girl, who was pretty
And thought he was some brand of animal. We'd sing
Their names together every chance we got, impressed

With her way of changing color, like some
Exotic lizard trying to disappear,
And forgot about Clifton pretty much till he came on us
Sudden one afternoon, wrathful and dumb
And swinging a length of cable. It wasn't fear

That defeated us. It was surprise
That it mattered so much what we'd done.
How could we know? He'd been one of us all our lives,
So close it was hard to see how he'd beat us
This once: he was already man enough to think he loved a woman.

So he came down on us sudden, boys,
All of us, and he gave us a taste of the hurt
We'd live to know another way: how love
Can be wrong and still be the only joy
That's real: how, when we come to it,

We stand amazed but take the blow, transfigured, idiot.

PASSION, CIRCUMSTANCE, WHAT I GAVE TO THE AIR

Not moonlight, starlight, or dawnlight: false dawn in no-color
Air of five A.M., uncentered, no shadows, the world
One shadow, one light. I have come here half-
Asleep, alone for the first time, hunting
Coat and gun too bright in the trees'
Luminescence to be anything but new.

September: big fox-squirrels chirr out of dark
Treetops, predawn. Leaves hang limp, stained at the dew point.
Groundfog clumps around oak-root snarls, and a small rain
Shatters down at a squirrel's jump: dew sparks
My blued rifle barrel. Hours from now, each drop
Will dry to a light spot of rust.

Old enough to be here now, tall enough to have to
Slap back low branches, cover my eyes,
I am ready. What my father showed me, what I know:
How to walk to woods' center, be still, wait
For what will give itself away above me,
What sound, what blur of body

Will tell me where to aim. But too soon: light
Does not come strong enough to show me the quick
Shape of flesh I will home in on. Alone in the vision
Mist gives me, I stumble my known way
To the dark old hickory my father says will hold
All I need. I settle in a silvered

Hollow of bole, cross my legs
With my long heft of rifle, lean back to wait, but fall
Asleep. In my dream the door opens, the room
Is dark, but I see the shape of the woman
Framed black in the bright doorway: the light
Behind her sparks her hair to white incandescence,

And she says my name. I do not know who she is,
But know that I will know, for the dream is clear
Prophecy, and when she comes toward me, I wake
Saying *Yes*, saying *Here*, reaching out in the empty
Morning that is not what it was: light slants
Hard from the east, trees throw dense shadows against

That brightness, and I am stiff in my jeans with a passion
I hardly know the name of. I am fourteen years old, and I touch
Myself there, try to think her face, try to see
Through darkness, through the blinding sweep
Of her hair. I see nothing, but I hear
From somewhere above me the hum I have heard before:

I stand, look for bees, see in a high
Hollow of hickory the mouth of a hive
Sealed over in the night with orb-spider web,
Fool of a spider dangling dead,
Stung to a withered nothing, bees trapped anyway,
Gold of their bodies struck in a shaft of sun,

A mass of dead bees scabbed
On dew-struck web: the whole hive pitched to a passion
Of madness. Still half dreaming, I feel
The rifle rise, hear the shot
Come out of great distance, know the light
Thrust of recoil on my shoulder is real as the bullet breaks

Deep into sweet comb, and wet web explodes with a swarming
Of gold, of wings sparked to diamond in the strong
Fall of morning: I stand with the gun still up,
Still aimed at the dark hive-hole,
As the hum dies away, and the day,
Second by second, in irreducible light, comes on.

—for Sydney Lea

THE PASSION OF THE RIGHT-ANGLED MAN

Halfway up, he sees it is morning, sees
Clouds turn neon red with florescence of dawn,
And suddenly he is sober. He would get down on his knees
If he were not where he is, and pray God to let it go on,
This arc-light shock the sky he is in is full of.
In the car below, they are laughing. The radio plays a song
About honky-tonks and passion, about some poor fool in love
With somebody gone. It's turned up loud. He hears the part
Where the son-of-a-bitch gets his face punched. Then he's above
Hearing any more. He's too high for that busted heart
To get to him, and he's getting higher. There is dawn, wind,
And the tower rises to the light that winks red, winks white
In the height he's climbing for, a warning, winks again and again
Endlessly, night and day. This was a dare,
But he forgets that, forgets the ground, the men
In the car down there who poured him full of bad beer
For hours to make him brave. And Lord, wasn't he brave
To mount that first rung with them laughing back in the car,
With that song on the radio there to make him believe
Love is wrong? Oh, yes, he was brave, but he went up anyway.
And now it's a long way down, that hurt he'll have to live
Sooner or later, when he's back on the ground—whole, they'll say,
And they'll laugh and go home. And he'll go home too, alone,
To the room where he suffers those dreams of her. But here, day
Has gone red to gold, he's sober, he wants to pray to someone
He doesn't believe in anymore not to make him go down:
To let some lonely woman miles away turn her TV on
And see him, patched in the signal this tower passes, grown
Whole on her screen, alive in the height of his passion,
Over the air and there for her, ninety degrees from the ground.

DAWN: WHAT I MIGHT HAVE DREAMED

It always has to begin
With sky, with whatever light
There is, a skirl of clouds:
Morning is there
And I have to care about it.
It is a letter someone sends

To a lover who never answers.
Out the window, past
The field I live at the edge of,
A farmer's wife
Is crying in her sleep.
The bedroom lightens,

Her husband wakes, sees
The tears again.
They pool in her closed eyes.
What can he do? It is the dream
She has had since childhood,
The one she will never

Speak of except to say
No, you were not in it.
It was not you.
He turns away, knows
She will not wake until it ends.
Everything in this light

Is far away, the cattle
In the field, the farmhouse on the hill,
But the light is very clear.
I see the door
Of the farmhouse darken,
See the small shape

Of the farmer come out.
He walks toward the barn
But stops in the open, stands
Still, then raises both arms
Toward the sky, where
In the illusion of great distances,

Two small planes, sunbursts,
Approach, collide.

TRAPS

They hurt me. I grow older.
—Pound

The gold bourbon-haze of my sleep
Slips, splits. There is something in the dark
And it bumps. I come out of no dream
To rise, stumble in the black
Tangle of sweat-damp pants
I cannot remember stripping
From the sourness of my legs,
But I do not fall. Holding on
To the slick-painted bedroom doorframe,
I hear it: the bump, the rattle:
A distant rhythm like music
In another room: and I am back
At the party, candlelight
A low glimmer on glass,
On tumblers, bottles moving
In half-dark, something slow
On a stereo—but no one
Is here, no light, no
Music but this chain-rattle off
Through the dark of my own
House I have come to not knowing,
Somehow in one piece.
There is first the shock of being
Awake, still half-drunk in darkness,
Then memory, a dull pain at the bottom
Of the skull: then, sudden,
The fear.

▪

The morning my neighbor showered down
With his twelve-gauge on a dog
Not thirty yards from the window
I slept on the other side of,
I was dreaming a woman's hand,

And the thunder it made on my face
Brought me stiff and awake.

I could see him on his house-trailer porch,
Barrel of the gun still level.
On the road parallel to us both,
Something white: he leaned the shotgun
On the wall, crossed lawn, lifted
The gut-ruptured mutt from the dust.

It hung by its legs upside down
In his hands, the hole in its side
Face-sized, rimmed ragged with bone.

He weighed it a second, then hefted it
Over barbed wire into the high
Grass of the landlord's pasture.
Turning back, he saw me, pale
O of my face in the window,
Raised his hand in a mock salute:

Chicken killer, he yelled at me.

Days later, in the light
Of October afternoon, I lofted
A fist-sized rock at that deep
Hollow in the grass, and they rose
Gold in a fog of distance, pairing:
Carrion butterflies.

▪

The witch sneaked up behind me
Where I leaned on a doorframe watching
A monkey fondle the tits
Of a jolly transvestite. I jumped.

Later the party was darker.
The apples were bitten, the punch
Spiked with Everclear swilled,
The pumpkin broken-faced, fallen
From a dance-shaken windowsill.

Satan in a red body stocking
Lay beautifully on the sofa,
Passed out, elastic leer
Hung by one scarlet band.

On the red shag rug around her,
Many body parts were scattered:
Ape-hands, mouse-tails, bird-feet,
And faces, faces, the eyes
Black, staring up at me

As I stomped across the room
Half drunk and wonderfully depressed.
Overhead, on a staircase, the monkey
Made sorrowful guitar noise.

He was playing my guitar.
I was in blackface, the blind
Street musician, holding a tin cup
Filled constantly to the brim
With cheap self-renewing bourbon,

And passing a mirror, I held it
Out to myself, said *Hey brother,*
Drop me some coins, I'll sing you
Some blues, said *Man, these honkies*

Got no soul. The face looked back at me,
Candlelight glinting on the dark
Lenses of a blind man's glasses,

And over its shoulder there floated
The ruined, stepped-on face

Of a hag, freak-wig hair
Sticking out of the black cone-hat.
Hey, said the witch voice, *that's my face*
You were walking on, sonny. I saw

The faces together, dark and pale
Ovals in the gold wing-beat
Of blown candles. The black face opened
Its mouth, teeth glinting white,
And I heard it over slow music:

Well, honey, you ought not laid it
Where a man's gonna put down his foot.

▪

On a night of black love, when the full
October moon lifted light
Over every drought-burnt field
In Oklahoma, I drove
My sad hulk of a car miles
To look for the silhouette
Of one respectable tree
Against that silver-smeared sky.
When I found it, I parked, leaned
Against it, cried like a fool
In love with somebody gone,
Felt a fool with my arms
Around a worm-eaten elm
Nobody would bother to burn.
I let go, touched the wet
Of my face, thought of her sweep

Of bright hair that would be,
In this light, no color I could name.

Coming home hours later, I saw
In my neighbor's barn lot beyond
My backyard fence, a fire
Built under a fifty-gallon drum
Set up on concrete blocks.
My neighbor stood by with a stick,
Stirred something steamy in the drum
Gone cherry-red with heat.
I walked to the fence. He nodded,
Dipped the stick in deep, pulled them out:
Black-jawed and ugly, they hung
By their chain from the stick's tip:
Varmit-traps, he said. *Got 'em laid*
All over. In the red lick of firelight,
They grinned, quiet-toothed and mean.
You gotta boil 'em, he said,
To get the dead smell off.

▪

And it comes again, and it comes:
That bump and rattle in the dark
Of October morning, so I stumble
To the back door, heart
Tight, switch on the porch light:
There, on the edge
Of vision, by the garbage cans, eyes
Blink bright: raccoon,
Its small mask-face turned
Toward me, struggles, left front paw
Locked in a black steel jaw
It found instead of trash-stink.
That bastard, I hiss, and I think

Of fields, dark hollows full
Of teeth anything might walk on,
Jaws everywhere. *My own
Damn yard*, I whisper,
Think myself so drunk
It is gone from my memory, my coming
Home from the party, falling
God knows where, my hand
In the slow motion
Of imagination jamming down
Where the raccoon's is now,
And now it is mine
To do, whatever I can do. What?
Kill it? Let it go?
I sway in the doorframe, put out
My hand, keep myself from falling.
The raccoon sees me move,
Panics, jerks twice,
Vanishes. I hear it rattle
In dry Johnson grass, then nothing:
And I breathe a long breath, grateful
For what has been taken from me.

▪

Inside, I grope back to bed.
I reach out in the dark, touch
Something strange, out of place, alive:
I jump back and cry out in my half-
Drunk fear, snap on the light:

She is there on the bed, naked, her name
Forgotten, her face
Smeared, a black bruise
Of mascara under one eye,

Too young, passed out, mouth open
In dead sleep, in a soundless
Snore, the dark inside
Framed by the white of teeth:
And I feel the wrong cut through me,
Wrong woman, oh, wrong life:
I run from the room, but stumble
On a dark pile of something:
Cape and cone-hat, empty-eyed
Stepped-on face: I fall
And do not rise again
Until dawn. Waked by the light,
I paw at my eyes,
My fingers come away

Black, and I go out remembering:
Find it there, crushed, chewed, torn off,
Left behind in the jaws, a small
Hand put out in the dark
Face of salvation: gone.

OR, IF YOU WERE CLOSER, I MIGHT TOUCH YOU

At dusk the hawk lifts, hangs black
Over white-green blossoms of milkweed.
It cries its old rusty cry.

Cattle vanish in a cloud
Of red dust whipped by the wind
The hawk breasts, floats on, rising.
In the mercy of this hazed light

I can tell myself no man
Has been here, ever,
No man and no woman walking

One in the shadow of the other.
This path is hoofmarked. I stumble
Trying to go home.
My hand goes out, blind,

Poor fool of a body believing
Someone is there,
But I do not fall. Going down,

I catch myself, I rise
Held up, somehow, on air.
The hawk, high in a cloudstroke,
Grows smaller, grows blacker, goes.

It is night now, the dark we held
Each other in, certain we cast
No shadow: but the cry of the hawk

Comes once out of nothing. Then nothing.
There is nothing between it and the light.

LOVE SONG

Bastard, I hear, and the sweep
Of the switchblade is blue in the light
Of the cobalt spot. I see the steel
Arc catch the dancer's side,

See his woman fall away and scream.
They face each other, the dancer,
The man with the knife.
Couples on the dance floor part:
The bass player stumbles,
The drummer throws down his sticks,
The saxophone is left

Playing all alone.
This is how long it takes:
The spotlight's color wheel
Has barely had time to turn
Blue to red, but the black-haired
Woman has screamed for hours
When the dancer takes his hands

Away from his belly, the middle
Of the right side, where they tell you
The appendix ought to be.
The stain, in that light colorless,
Starts to grow. I cannot stop

The music coming
Out of the horn without me,
Vibrato trembling in my jaw
As the dancer goes down on one knee:

The other man bends over him.
The light shifts red to yellow,
The blade of the knife blazes brass,

The man who holds it stands staring
At the man who kneels staring back,

And I cannot stop that music,
Though nobody touches, nobody dances,
Nobody sings a word.

THE LOST WOMAN

In noon light the wheat, brass-bright,
Bristles in the field, no wind
To open it. The woman is walking
Waist deep. In that shimmer

Of July air, she has only a shape,
No face he can put a name to.
He jerks back the throttle, feels

The tractor under him stall
With the suddenness of his stopping,
With something that is rising

In his throat, a word, *who:*
But the silence of the strangled engine
Ripples over the field.
Behind him in the long

Swath of windrow, nothing moves,
Nothing moves in the air

But heat at the woman's waist
Where she is cut in half by the line
Of wheat against sky. He is still

Caught in the rattle of morning,
Roar and buck of the tractor,
Silver *clip* of the cutter-bar:

His body hums in the quiet.
His hands tingle, touching

Hot metal as she walks
From nowhere, disappearing
Toward nothing he knows,
And he stands up, wanting her

To turn, see him there, held
High against the bright
Summer sky, stopped dead

In the middle of everything, trying
To wave, trying to call,
The *hey* stuck in his throat
Something that might have been

Where did you come from
Love, oh, where have you gone?

II

LOVE POEM

The Obsessed

Scattering leaf-chaff
From the whine of blade,
A mower turns
Its littered yard
Clear. This is one

Of the rituals of love,
This wasp-rotation
Of small machine
Caught in its own

Impossible corner
Of quick-mulched lawn,
Each swath a dim
Imitation of windrow,
As though in the deep

Mind, an image
Of field takes hold
And everyone plows
Whatever shape

Of blade he possesses
Into the heaped
Fall leaves of his land.
These are the houses
Of love I walk by,

Raising my hand
To meet the raised hands
Of husbands, who live
Strange-shaped lives

In the clean planes
Of yards they pay for,
And the hands of wives

With their rakes and trowels
Bought for the beds

Of bulbs they turn
To find the odd
Clumps and bulges
Of next year's iris,

Kind women, looking up
To wave at a stranger.
These are the streets
Love dreams of, where
Children come

With their names in the gathering
Dusk, to call
Words incomprehensible
To anyone from anywhere

Else but here,
Anyone who cannot
Judge what passion
Asks of these
Who labor, turning

To each other in the dark
Of yards, having
Done what is called for,
Knowing it is good.

GENEALOGY

3rd of July, Salt Lake City

Some poor son-of-a-bitch's poor son-of-a-bitch
Of a son just took the last six-pack
Down from the shelf, and every grocery store in town
Closes in five minutes. His family tree
Is at my mercy. He's a jack-Mormon, I can tell
By my anger: I want him to be.
I want his great-grandmother out on the desert half-dead
Of supernatural thirst to see her seed
Has come to this. I want those patient teetotaling souls
In heaven to know who they're waiting for.
I want his history to suffer.

Outside in the parking lot, I watch the store go dark
A minute early by my watch, eleven fifty-nine,
Not midnight by a long shot. With arc-lights gone,
Stars come out sudden, and in sudden starlight this town,
Stopped dead by a holiday, glitters. I think of water,
Midnight by the pond, a flash of matchlight, my father
Waving a cigarette, talking, the red arc
Of the tossed match ending in a hiss. The story
He told me is gone, but I know he sleeps
Quieter in his far time zone for what he does not know
Of me, what I thirst for, what I love, what I have done
To what he would have sworn was only history.

CORRESPONDENCE: FADED LOVE

As I look at the letters that you wrote to me
It's you that I'm thinking of. . . .

—Bob Wills

. . . his lyrics were generally romantic, unrealistic,
and lacked . . . honesty. . . .

—Charles R. Townsend, "Homecoming:
Reflections on Bob Wills and His
Texas Playboys, 1915–1973"

For George Woodward and Nannie Carlisle: lovers and correspondents: married 1856

▪

Thin grandmotherish snow
Skims over the flat
Parallels of Oklahoma,
Scums the window

And the bush outside the window white:
The distance between them pales.
I want to say
In the letters I write you

What it profits a man to lose all
The world and only
Gain his soul. I want you
To know the truth about love: how thin

It is, how it obscures
What it touches so
The cardinal on the wind-
Struck limb outside is caught

Between nothing and nothing,
And the white horse standing
Snowbacked in the barn lot
Can vanish without ever moving.

▪

George Woodward, my uncle
Four times great
And a hundred-some years removed,
Wrote *Dear Nannie: I am well*

And pray you are the same, wrote
Nannie, I regret
We are not better acquainted—we
Could then throw off

Any restraint.
He wrote from Louisville, Kentucky
To Nannie, at home
In Mississippi, of *restraint.*

I have his letters: twenty
Faded, tight-folded, tiresome,
Overwritten, quaint
Installments attesting to the passion

Of George Y. Woodward for one
Nannie Carlisle, who is forever
Silent, her letters in return
Lost. He wrote: *Oh Nannie, please write soon.*

▪

I want to tell you a story.
The truth is, there is no story,
There is only the wanting to tell.
The truth is, there is only

Me, watching the window to see
How long it will take the light
To vanish altogether.
The truth: the light is all there is.

George to Nannie: *Saturday night*
I had my "likeness" taken: the photographer
Near blinded me with his flash.
It is not a very good one, but will do.

I send it with this letter.
With this letter, I would send the pale wash
Of evening snowlight to you,
Would send you what I see:

My hand on the desk: the blue
Paper he wrote to her on: the white
It pleases me to use, fading slowly
With snowfall: it is no good story, but will do.

▪

This much is lost: the tintype
He had made: what she thought
Of how he looked, so far away
So long: your face, wiped

Clean out of my mind. What
Time and space do not take,
Light wants: I remember
Only what I can see.

Nannie, forgive me if I speak
Rashly: I gaze often on your
Likeness, your face:
Oh, it is a great

Pleasure to behold an eye
As beautiful as thine! Time, space,
The slow fading of light:
Truth is, memory

Is nothing. What is lost
Is the shape of a face, the hand
That touched it. Truth is what I see
In the window's mirror, fading: myself, ghost.

▪

Backed with the silver-white
Of snow, the window shines
In the room's dusk,
A trick of circumstance, false dawn, light

Not found in the world. Imagine
Yourself nowhere.
Imagine a place that is not a place,
Light that is not light

But memory, trying to make something be there.
Imagine you love a face
You'd swear you've never seen.
That is what distance is, that

Trying to imagine.
I am lost in this room, shut in
By the truth: what
Touches me is real.

All that touches me is snow, night.
The silence fools me: I believe
If I put my hand out, I would feel
Nothing. I reach for the light.

■

Nannie, forgive me for writing
So long a letter: I hope it
Will not weary you to read.
Do as I have done in writing:

Read part of it,
Eat your dinner, then read on.
Nannie, I fear I cause you
Pain, writing as I do:

I mean to cause no pain:
I want to write to you
Honestly. My feelings are sensitive,
I cannot help it well

What I say. I know
You understand, and will forgive.
I want to tell
You this: I wished to see you

The morning I left, came to your door,
But could not knock. Ah, Nannie, it is well:
I could not see you weep, or wish you to.
Be happy. I will speak of it no more.

■

No more: the dark
Clicks backward: the desk lamp glows.
The room is a room.
All this talk

Is wrong: start again. The window
Is blank. I raise it, shake
The screen. Snow-scum shatters:
The horse in the barn lot is a white

Startled blur. The snow is done. I take
One long breath of clear air,
Shut the window again.
I want to tell you a story:

I am lost somewhere in Oklahoma,
Sitting in a room alone
Thinking, like a fool, I can say
Something about love you will believe:

That over the dark barn lot
Stars break free of clouds, gleam:
That the world is real. *Nannie, forgive. . . .*
I am weary. . . . I did not mean. . . . Oh, I cannot. . . .

▪

George to Nannie: *I have come to know*
The doctor's life is a hard one:
We labor to get the skill
Of healing, then harder after: I go

Among the Irish, who cannot pay: I learn.
What was his face like: the likeness
Lost to us? I would tell you
If I knew: tired

With long hours, lean smile held too
Careful for the slow burn of lens?
I saw a magnificent balloon
Go up two days ago.

Six men went up with it. I should like
To go also: it would soon
Bring me to you if the wind would blow
Aright, but today it is from the south.

I would tell you how he looked, body
Tilted to follow the bright, slow climb
Of the airship in that wrong wind, both
Of us tense, testing the clear air, lonely:

▪

I would tell you everything:
How they came together, touched,
Married, raised children, died:
How history happened: how hard I cling

To this story: how much
Of it is lies.
I will tell you what I know:
It is late. It is cold.

The snow crusts over: hard freeze.
You are not with me, so
I will sleep alone. That much is true.
Whatever else I say, suspect me.

I twist my desk lamp, beam it
Over, out the window:
In the ice-bush, light blazes: I see
Shadows stab suddenly

Onto blankness of snow.
That much: world's light, shadow.
I set the lamp down softly,
Turn on the radio.

▪

Clearing and colder. Tonight
No more snow. There will be
Distance, there will be dark.
Sunrise at six. You might

Be wise to stay up for it: probability
For vision is high:
Sunlight on snow will burn you where you stand.
Nannie, you always fear the worst,

That this winter will be hard: but I
Have hope for the future. Hope. I scan
The stations: music
From Tulsa: "Faded Love."

I listen close, can hear
Faint wordless static
Pitched just above
The sweep of steel guitar.

It is true, that old
Hiss of blown snow on ice.
Love, I will write you another letter
All my life: my lying human voice:

Don't listen. Love the other
Empty voice that is the world.

TRAIN WRECK, 1890: MY GRANDMOTHER LIES DOWN WITH THE DEAD

You come to in the past, dark, where the fires still burn
Hot enough in the wreck of the tender to turn iron
Bright, and that red light hovers over the bodies

Heaped just down the embankment—waking, you
Remember only the dream you were having an hour ago,
Asleep on your father's lap in half-dark, dead

Of morning. What was the dream? The porter
Passes quietly in gas-light, sees the right hand
Of the small girl, draped on the fat man's lap, clench.

The fat man is sleeping too, his head lolled
At a broke-neck angle onto the woman's shoulder.
The woman is awake. She takes your hand,

Unrolls the fingers gently. You were holding on
To something in your dream. The porter smiles
At white people's human love, thinks of his own

Granddaughter, tips his cap, goes down
The aisle toward the club car he will never come to.
Coming to, you can only open one eye. Above you

On the slope, coal from the tender smokes thick,
And you think you see men running. Where you are
It is quiet, dark, everything is a long way off

But the dream. You jerk
When the porter slams the door. Your mother
Touches your hair, speaks a word, inaudible, her hand

On your face, in love, in your sleep. She is looking
At your black sweep of hair, delicate twitch
Of eyelids: knows you dream, knows you see

What you will never tell her, something shaken
Out of you by the rattle of the coach, the touch
Of the hand you do not wake to. She leans

Over you, squints at your face, traces,
Not touching skin, the line of your jawbone—
It is not in your dream, the distance of breath

Her fingers are from your face. You will not remember
The hard wonder she stares down at you the moment before
Something breaks deep in the line, the dark you come to

Alone, burned in the shadow of smoke and the lap of the dead
Stranger strange men find you next to, men who lift you,
Look hard in your face, lay you down, believing you

Will never open your eyes in this iron-light of the tender,
Never tell them who, in the black plunge of love,
You belong to again.

THE ORACLE OF THE LONELY MAN IN STILLWATER, OKLAHOMA

Some man's semi-beautiful daughter
Lays her warm hands under the table
On the leg of a boy who might be
Me, grown suddenly young
And stupid with the unexplainable rising
Of passion in a public place.
It happens again and again.
Every restaurant, every bar I go to
They are there in their different bodies,
Merciless in the half-dark, touching
As though my being here,
Ex-husband, would-be father,
Makes them want me to see them reach
Over whatever distance is left
And hold each other hard
In the world's knowing:
As though that knowing were mine.
I drink, I watch them move
On a dance floor or out the door,
But with me always, coming
And going in whatever light
There happens to be, whispering
Each others' names over and over,
Not knowing what they are saying:
The way they might touch and name
The strange inner organs
Of beasts and fowls.

—for Bob Campbell

THOSE, TRESPASSING

From overland, from the far
And out of sight house
Where my mother and father
Sleep in the pond-hazed peace
Of this Sunday dawn,
I am coming, the kiss

Of dew-silvered April-long
Grass at my knees,
And in my hand the stolen
Rod. It whips, whistles:
Long in my hand, it is light
And subtle as a snake's tongue, it is

High-polished, fine-balanced, it
Is costly, a gift of love
A woman gave a man—and if he caught
Me with it now, he'd give me
Hell, but what he doesn't know
In his sleep can't hurt me. I wave

That intricate lightness in a false throw,
And the silver lure of my passion
For the hard leap of a hooked fish goes
Nowhere, quivers on
The sensitive tip.
I follow the fish-shaped shine

Of the lure down the east slope
Of pasture, thigh-wet
With dew, walking light toward the drop
Of dam, the slip where the boat
Lies locked
By a steel-bright

Chain to the trunk
Of a water-oak. I have the key
In a pocket, picked
Silent, on the sly,
From my father's ring. I reach
In for it, take it, hold it ready

In my palm's sweat, leg-heat
Live in the metal, burning MASTER,
Steel-etched brand-name letters, deep
In the dark of my clenched hand. Not far
Now to the fallen gate,
The easy step over rain-rotted barbed wire,

The oak, the locked boat,
The water. I am coming blind
In water-silvered brilliance of dawnlight,
Then sudden black of eclipse behind
The etch-scaped trunk of the oak.
I lay my hand

On old roughness of bark,
Feel for the cold of chain: I find it
Fallen low, slack,
Lockless, boatless, empty-ended.
For a moment the pure shock
Of its vacant weight

Is fear: then I pull it back,
Hold it up, let it hang
Too light, broken in my hand like
Line snapped by a fish-lunge.
Something is gone, and I think
Wrong, wrong,

Think the boat sunk,
Think chainbreak. I drop it and lean
Around the scored trunk,
Stare down at the pond's dawn-sheen,
All surface, hazed water too bright
To see into. And then

I look up, out:
He is there, a dark man-shape
Riding the boat's silhouette
Over the milk of mist, pole-slope
A spear-thin line
Thrust out of his chest, angled up,

Skyward. I hold my hand
To shade my eyes, try to see
His face, think *How can*
It be, how could he—
But no, it is not my father,
He has not beaten me

Here, it is someone else, some stranger,
Trespasser, lock-picker, come to poach
Our fish: my fish. The anger
Is a quick heat in my belly. I stretch
From behind the oak, ready
To call him down, but feel breath catch

In my throat as the woman suddenly
Comes out of willows on the far
Side of the pond. She raises an arm, silently
Signals, and I know her:
Cotton-chopper, maid,
Floor-scrubber: I think *Nigger*

What're you doing as the man turns his head
And lifts his hand to her. He lays
His pole on the gunwale, dips his oar-blade:
No, not his,
My father's, mine:
And the boat turns, soundlessly goes

Toward her, runs aground
In soft mud of the shallows.
Black in that strong sun,
He stands, steps in water I know
Is inches deep, but it by God looks
From where I am like he floats

Across to her, like he walks
On that fine impenetrable sheen
Of sun-sparked mist on water, and he takes
Her in his arms, is her husband:
I see I know him, too:
Tenant, my father's hand,

Face visible now in the shadow
Where he holds her. He holds her the way
I know men do:
His hands move: they
Step back into the trees, are,
In that deeper shade, one body,

And I think *God, where*
Have I seen this before?—then know,
Think *No, not them*, but my mother and father
Are the same, love is the same, and I turn, go
Stumbling away down the bank, face
Burned with what I have come to,

Not shame or knowledge but loss
Of more than I knew I thought was mine:
And when I fall I do not break
The rod, but I lose without knowing it is gone
The key, its backward name on the flesh
Of my hand fading as I scramble up, go on

To the house where my parents lie in the black hush
Of unknowing, holding each other still, in sleep, precious,
Robbed, blind.

DROWNING

A Ghost Story

I want to see it: the window
Emptied even of starlight,
Curtains invisible—no pale
Prayer-cloth-flappings in wind—there
Is not even wind. A window in the dead

Dark: nothing anyone could see,
So I go there blind, where my mother,
A girl, lies staring,
Not knowing she stares, her eyes
The same, closed or open, the power

Of her hearing huge
In the night, grown as far
As the river a mile away. It is deep
Summer, July. I am in the room
So quietly that she hears through me

The slow moving of water,
The current's roll breaking
On bridge-pilings, opening, closing.
She hears. She lies still.
She cannot sleep for wanting

The clap of an oar on water,
The grind of a boat-keel dragged
On the sandbar, the laughter
Of men half-drunk on the river,
Faint, their voices wordless

But known. I put my hand
Out in blackness, touch
Nothing. I cannot see
Where the bed is. Her face
Is out of reach. All I know

Is what she will say
Years later: they will not come,
The fathers, will never drift
Downriver on the tide they bucked
Daylong in the burning

Sun of July and the joy
Of the bottle they passed in their rowing.
I know they will not come,
She will not hear them talking, parting,
Never hear the slap

Of a hand on a shoulder, the quiet
Goodbyes. It is night, it is summer,
The window is somewhere, the sound
Of the river comes through,
A long, unbroken rhythm:

And maybe my mother sleeps
Without knowing she sleeps,
Maybe she dreams
She hears the heavy footsteps
Of a man risen up from the water,

A man who would glitter in moonlight
If there was a moon, a man
Who sings to himself an old song
Of rivers, his clothes
Gone strange, full of the smell

Of where he has been: he opens
The gate, she hears him
Singing, not whiskey now on his breath,
And she strains in the dark to see him
Through the window, but there is no window,

No man, no song.
Maybe she never slept.
How can I know? In the silence
Of years, I cannot even hear
Her breathing. I am alone

In any dark place, I am a boy
Waking in the night, lungs full
Of fever and the river-water
Of asthma, I am drowning
On the sickbed in my parents' room

While they sleep not ten feet away
And the March wind ticks
Oak-limbs on the window,
Invisible: someone is lost
In a slow, dark current,

But, oh, it is not me,
It has no face, no name,
It is going nowhere, and I scream
Without making a sound
Till my mother comes without waking

To touch me. I cannot see
Her hand, but I hold to it, hold it hard
As she brings me back
To the breath that grinds in my chest
And I am in the world, having been here

All this time to come
Dark to my mother: I am not
Even a pale radiance in this night
Before I was born: not even
The light of my knowing can show me

My mother's face.
It is only a day since her father
Took his pole and his oar to the river.
She cannot know they will never
Find even the oar. Let me tell her

Mother, you have not lost him,
Let me touch her, keep her
Out of time, out of everything
She will give up to bring me screaming
From darkness to the pure burning

Joy of my new breath,
Shining wet in the light,
Dragged up by strange hands, alive.

LOVE'S MERCY AND THE DARK WORLD DYING

We hear the barking in our sleep
And sleep on hearing, turning
Clenched faces to the shadows
Of walls: we keep our breathing
Slow: but it goes on
Into the ice-bright clarity
Of February dawn
Until our father takes his rifle down
And echoes that call

Over the frost-burnt field.
When the breath of his calling
Pillars white in the air,
We come: and the three pointers come
Torn over that quarter mile
Of mastered ground between
The dark line of hedgerow and the yard,
Come hot-eyed and high-strung, quivering
Under our hands as we speak their names,
My brother and I still thick-tongued
From the hard sleep we willed
Hours in the voice-shaken night:
They neither answer
To what we call them, nor stay
To be touched:
                                        they shake us off
Where we stand half dumb
By the door: they run to take
The back gate in leaps
Fine-boned as quail-flight.
We hear them raise
Their baying as we look
In the dark of closets for coats,
Listen as we follow
Our father's rifled shadow
Through the gate into pasture:

Down there, in the hedgerow, something:
Knowledge needing no more saying
Than this winter of dawnlight
We take the field in, filed
By instinctive order of age,
My father, my brother, me,
Their bigger bodies equal
To mine in what all bodies know.
We cross that cold-cracked ground
And come to the old double row
Of bois d'arc trees arched high
And black:
                        it is now some dream
Might return to me out of the long
Tongue-broken sleep, some clear
Voice out of memory or that mind
We share unspoken on the edge
Of these bole-warped shadows,
But only the panicked pitch
Of the dogs comes, and we go on
Into the hall these trees
Wall on each side of our fence line,
Shade here so dense
Not even briars grow
Up the barbed wire rusted black
On its rotted twists of post wood.
My father stops, stands
Still, leaning, listening,

And we hear it under
Hound-noise: the other
Sound, a single note tuned so high
It is almost beyond hearing,
But not beyond: is there: I feel
Flesh knot on my spine
As somebody whispers *Jesus*, somebody runs:

Running, I suddenly see
The white of dogs' bodies circling
In the dark ahead, bristling,
Crazy, held back
By the one pure sound
A deer can make:
                                        and I see it there
On the barbed wire, hung
Where it tried to jump but missed
The top fence strand,
The scream rising
As it jerks at my coming.
I kneel to see
Both front legs broken clean
At the shoulders, a sliver of light
Bone thrust through
Shadow-stain of hide:
It goes on, that sound
Out of nowhere, out
Of the dark morning is.

I put my hand
On its throat, but cannot feel
That voice. The deer quivers,
Twists: my father is there
With his rifle behind me
To catch my wrist, shake his head:
Nothing is said, nothing
Needs saying:
                                  but my brother and I,
In the field now, in the light
Of this memory, wait
For the breath that will give us back
The world's silence: stand called
In the resonance of air
To know the echo

Of that cold syllable's mercy, recoiling
Out of our father's hands
In its singular dream of pain.

—for Alexis Khoury

CIRCUMSTANCE: THE VANISHING

Light in this house of pain
Is so ice-clear you think
There must be snow. But when
You turn to the window, it is still

Oklahoma evening, cloudless autumn.
Or that is what I think you think
As I watch you turn. In the hall,
White carts click

Newborns from the nursery toward rooms
Where whole generations wait,
Arms out for the small
Time bomb of body

They have given their meaningless names.
But here we are nameless, here
We hold on to the frayed
End of the rope of flesh

Wondering what broke
And into what dark.
Not priest or doctor
Or brother, I have no right

To anything but the words
Friends speak, nothing that gives
Reasons, and I thank whatever passes
For God: I have felt the near-

Invisible shiftings of the things of this world
And not known what to call them.
Here, it is far too easy to feel
Sanctimonious or certain:

In this clear white light
I find I think I know
Too much, am ready to believe
Any continuity. So I say

Nothing, and in my silence I slip
Back years, assume again the body
Of the boy who wakes in the brilliance
Of November morning, tangled

In his life, who runs
Downstairs to find his mother and father
Gone, and the grim grandmother
Holding her arms low to him in her black love

To gather him and his silent brother
Into the car. In the backseat, looking
At the roll of his grandmother's hair
Done up in a bun and fastened

With a silver cross-headed pin,
The boy begins to shake
For no reason he can name:
None has been given, and the boy

Will not know for years that his mother lies
Pale on the white bed in the name of his sister
Who died with a sudden twist in the womb
Five months gone in her dark life:

Who would have been
The third child of that good woman
But could not live for something
Negative in the blood

That all the doctors say
By every law of reason and statistics
Kills each child after the first.
But the boy does not even know

That he shakes because the cross
Pinned to the gray of his grandmother's hair stirs
Part of him back to the day
A month before, when his brother,

Four years older and wise,
Pointed vaguely toward cloudy sky,
Said *Everybody dies. And you go up there.*
Looking, the boy saw nothing

But a bright antenna nailed
To the rooftop. His brother told him
You have to go
All by yourself. And you never

Come back. The boy stared up
At that silver T of metal,
Believing, not believing,
Feeling a nameless

Outrage of loss grow in his belly, crying
No, I won't,
I'm staying here.
But his brother, metaphysician

Of the rational, shook his head,
Said *Think what you want.*
When it's time, you go.
And now this strange

Silent ride is a beginning
Of years he will not understand
Where he is going, why nobody speaks
Of the sister who lived

Her little time because of the hope
His life was, the second son
Born by a miracle
Of miscalculation, a blip

In the law of averages, surviving
Day after day in the wonder of his flesh
That slipped from his mother blue
With death-smell, to sit

Here now with others who have lost
More than he knows, not knowing
What to say to them.
But that is too easy, too,

So we talk awhile of things
That make no difference.
I leave you staring out
Into the lie of light, believing

You will watch me cross
The parking lot, a small
And disconnected figure
Who dropped in out of the world, alive,

Spared in the outrage of love, to tell you
Nothing true: gone when you slip
Into the night your child
Turned sharp in its dark world of body,

The blood-rope twisted wrong.

—for Michael and Diane Bugeja

FLYING AWAY

You and I, we make a separate world.
—D. H. Lawrence

Which long way is home when the airplane breaks
Whatever *sound barrier* means and carries me
Out of the cloud of snow I touched you in?
West of your city, sun for the first time in days:
Thirty-nine thousand feet below, light stars
Ice fields beside the long meander of the Mississippi.
I am the stupid passenger, the numb one, the patient
Who does what he is told: *seat-back up, please.*
It is hard to know why I am here when there is no *here.*
It is hard to remember this is an act of love.

Wound, vein, scar: clichés for river. From this high,
The Mississippi is nothing I can name,
A zone of translucence between two brilliant sheets,
Bodiless, like the opaque trail I know
This jet must be leaving behind me. Murmur of engines
Is all that reaches me, felt, not heard, through the arms,
The uprightness of my seat. *Where are you now? Now?*
Do you still feel the near-imperceptible brunt
Of wind on walls in the night, hear the unreal
Rattle of snow? They will give me whatever I want,

Coffee, whiskey, clear ice in a cup I can hold
Up to the window, shatter the light. They will tell me
Where I am going: *Oklahoma. Home.* There's a place
Down there where a pond's gone dry: you can stand
In a circle of willows and stare, as long
As your neck has strength, at a ragged circle of sky,
Always clear, pale, this year of drought.
Sooner or later, half-seen, something will move
In that blue. Darker? Lighter? Focus:
It is colorless, hawk or plane or trick

Of the eye, dust, nothing. It is hard
To see when everything is too clear.
Rattle of ice in a cup: small sunburst on the far

Wall of the plane, on the face of someone asleep,
Politician, businessman, a stranger. I turn
The cup, project my fragments
Of sun until he stirs, brushes at his eyes. *Snow*
In the pale sweep of your hair: you touch my face,
Brush snow away. Maybe I make him dream
Of a point in the sky, something flying

Away from him, flamelike, bright with my touch of light.
I turn the cup again. He settles, snores.
Leaving you, I am blinding in his dream
Of home, children, wife: I am something clear,
Half-seen in the noon sky over the Midwest, turning
Neither wrong nor right but *other* in this hard love
That makes me go. He sees, he does not see,
He turns his face away, not wanting to know
What touches him, not hearing me when I say
It's all right, friend. Sleep. We live apart.

GOING IN

A Prayer for the Others

Off yonder, in those far houses,
They are touching
Their sleeping children,
They are talking, not too loudly,
Not of anything in particular,
Whatever comes to mind.
Wind shuffles maple leaves over windows.
There, where people say
They love each other
And lay their children down,
Somebody opens a door.
I see the oblong light
Flick across the yard.

From this hillside,
From the second fork of an oak
Where I have climbed
In darkness, I can see
Many houses,
Windows, lights, shades, shadows
Moving past curtains drawn
Against people like me.
I want to tell them all
I would only look in kindness,
Without judging, only see
Sheets rising light
With the daughters' breathing:

And in that one yard
Where light cantilevers out,
The man and woman appear.
They are walking, looking at stars.
If I passed them now, they would
Speak to me, I know it,
On their way inside
To lie down together,

Love each other, sleep.
They are a long way off.
I cannot hear what they are saying.
As they pass back and forth
Through the light, the woman's hair shines.
It is silver, no, gold,
And the man touches it quickly.

So what would I say
For them, what would I ask?
If their lives
Were what I imagine, there would be
Something impossible in the world,
Like a man
In a tree late at night, where no
Grown man ought to be:
A man who would look
Like a fool if anyone saw him,
But nobody will, so he sits
Quiet, watching, saying
To himself again and again
Yes, I love a woman too.
I am going in.

SORROW

When my grandmother was dying
She could forget
Everything she hated,
How my grandfather laid
His hard farmer's hands on her
And wrung out sons:
How she loved her sons,
But how bitter the act of love was,
Why she was a dark
And melancholy woman.

Maybe joy is a matter of losing
Your earthly connections,
Maybe only then can you love
Clean, without hatred or desire.
Once when I was a boy
I was walking in woods
I thought I knew, near dusk,
And suddenly everything went strange,
The light, the leaves on the ground:
Shadows pointed east
So I walked west, the way
I thought I had to go,
But nothing came clear,
Nothing but sunlight burning
Through oaks, blinding me
Until I found the shadow
Of one trunk to walk in:
I followed it, came
To a young tree, took it
In my hands
Like a woman's waist,
Forgot to be afraid, not caring
As long as I held on.

My mother told me this:
When my grandmother was dying,
She turned to a nurse
And asked *Are you my child?*
The nurse said *No.*
My grandmother took her hand,
Held on hard: whispered *Well*
It doesn't matter then.
It's all right.
Yes. All right.

A KINDNESS

Pink-spattered white, the shattered
Wing trails circles in the dust
Of the driveway where the bird dog
Goes for the egret's throat.
In clear March dawn light
The bird spreads its one good wing
Suddenly wide, star-white, splits
The gold of its beak, and screams.
I come out on the porch, see the dog
Stop cold and crouch, consider
Wing-weight and the point
Of the spike-thin bill.
The egret turns to fix
One eye, colorless and strange,
On the dog. The grass is dark
Around its feet. I can see
A hole the size of my fist
In the pit of the stained,
Limp-hung, trembling wing.
Now the dog subtly gathers
A half-inch lower: the bird
Throws its head back, neck
White as the dream of a girl's thigh,
And again, out of the gut-shot
Bellows of its body, the scream
Is torn. God's mercy, it is high
And lonely as an angel, set white
On the long grave of its shadow,
And I feel it rise,
The breath in my throat, not knowing
What it is, command,
The word.

LOVE POEM

The Dispossessed

In March, the small river,
Gray in the heart
Of your small gray city,
Thaws. I am cold
In this northern wind.
The part of the world
I come from would not know
What to call this gray

Stone wall I walk on.
There, they would name it
Levee. Snow
Banks in the deep
Shadow below me. Sun
Will get to it
Weeks from now, I guess,
But there are many things here

I would not try to predict:
When these strict silver
Trees will put their names
On with their leaves:
Gray, they are all
One tree to me,
Winter, the cold
Scum-white roil

Of river-water,
The high sweet call
Of a bird I cannot see,
Have never thought of.
I have walked
A long way in your cold
City where I should not be,
Thinking *cold*, thinking *love*,

Following the margin,
Skirting broken stones
In the wall that holds back
This river no one knows
I am walking beside alone,
Your river I cannot write down
The name of, can never
Say I was here beside

In this life, this time
Of year. I move
Slowly with the wind
From left to right, a small
Figure in an old
Photograph on the back
Of a postcard, black and white,
Mailed years ago:

Years lost
In the small post office
Of an obscure Southern town,
A gray thing come to light
Unsigned in your mailbox:
A dim winter
Scene of how this city
Looked a life ago.

The river has broken out
Of its winter ice a block
From the nameless motel
I have let myself in for,
A place it is hard to live
The good love that will not let me
Write down the things we know, the words
We call each other by.

Above me, high in the silver
Light, you can just make out
The dark shape of an unknown
Bird that hangs on the wind.
God knows who sent it.
God knows why
Anyone would bother
To forward such a thing.

POETRY FROM ILLINOIS

History Is Your Own Heartbeat
Michael S. Harper (1971)

The Foreclosure
Richard Emil Braun (1972)

The Scrawny Sonnets and Other Narratives
Robert Bagg (1973)

The Creation Frame
Phyllis Thompson (1973)

To All Appearances: Poems New and Selected
Josephine Miles (1974)

Nightmare Begins Responsibility
Michael S. Harper (1975)

The Black Hawk Songs
Michael Borich (1975)

The Wichita Poems
Michael Van Walleghen (1975)

Cumberland Station
Dave Smith (1977)

Tracking
Virginia R. Terris (1977)

Poems of the Two Worlds
Frederick Morgan (1977)

Images of Kin: New and Selected Poems
Michael S. Harper (1977)

On Earth as It Is
Dan Masterson (1978)

Riversongs
Michael Anania (1978)

Goshawk, Antelope
Dave Smith (1979)

Death Mother and Other Poems
Frederick Morgan (1979)

Local Men
James Whitehead (1979)

Coming to Terms
Josephine Miles (1979)

Searching the Drowned Man
Sydney Lea (1980)

With Akhmatova at the Black Gates
Stephen Berg (1981)

More Trouble with the Obvious
Michael Van Walleghen (1981)

Dream Flights
Dave Smith (1981)

The American Book of the Dead
Jim Barnes (1982)

Northbook
Frederick Morgan (1982)

The Floating Candles
Sydney Lea (1982)

Collected Poems, 1930–83
Josephine Miles (1983)

The River Painter
Emily Grosholz (1984)

The Passion of the Right-Angled Man
T. R. Hummer (1984)